SVEN & OLE JOKES,

AND MORE

CARLTON CARNEY

Printed in the United States of America.

Library of Congress Control Number: 2018967403

ISBN	Paperback	978-1-64361-401-4
	eBook	978-1-64361-402-1

Westwood Books Publishing LLC
10389 Almayo Ave, Suite 103
Los Angeles, CA 90064

www.westwoodbookspublishing.com

INTRODUCTION

Humor, in one form or other, has been part of my life from the early beginning. My Dad always had a humorous tale to tell. Much of his pastime was spent reading joke books, or listening to comedy radio shows, then later, comedy television. He could take everyday events and find humor in them. He had a sharp mind and a good memory, enabling him to tell jokes and stories upon request. I guess a little of that rubbed off on me.

As for Sven and Ole, they are popular with the large Scandinavian population in the Minnesota-Wisconsin region of the United States, just as Pat and Mike jokes are popular with the large Irish population in and around the Boston area. I like to think of these pairs as their region's Dumb and Dumber. As for which is Dumb and which is Dumber, that's for you to decide.

Hoping this book brings many smiles to your faces and money to my wallet.

Carlton Carney

A LONG WALK

One day Sven was out for a walk when he met Ole. He asked Ole if he knew where a certain convenience store was located. Ole didn't know but walked over to a stranger and asked if he knew about the store.

"Did he know vere da store located?" Sven asked as Ole returned.

"Ya, he say it straight ahead, but it a long valk," Ole answered.

"Dat okay," Sven replied, "I vill jog dere."

"Too bad you not have a bike, it be even shorter distance," Ole commented.

SVEN'S RIDDLE

"I have da riddle for you, Ole," Sven said.

"Okay, vut da riddle?" Ole asked.

"Brudderes or sisters, I have none but dis person is my fadder's son. Who is it?" Sven asked.

Ole repeated it several times. "I don't know," Ole said. "Who is it?"

"It's me," Sven announced.

"Say dat pretty good, I gonna say da riddle to Lars," Ole said.

Ole goes over to Lars' home, sees him in the yard, and says he has a riddle for him. "Brudders or sisters, I have none but dis person is my fadder's son. Who is it?"

Lars thought about it and then said, "That vould be you, Ole."

"Ha, I got you good, Lars, da answer is Sven," Ole proudly announced.

HOW BIG IS A FOREST?

"Say Ole, I have a riddle for you," Sven said.

"Ya, vut da riddle?" Ole asked.

"How big is a forest?" Sven asked.

"Vut forest you talk about? Da von behind your house?" Ole asked.

"Any forest. Da answer good for any forest," Sven said smiling.

"I don't know answer for any forest," Ole said. "How big is a forest, smarty-pants?"

"It twice as far as to da middle," Sven proudly answered. "And same riddle good for anything, like a city, a lake or even a farm."

"I go see if da vife can figure dis riddle," Ole smiled.

"Say, Lena, I has da riddle for you," Ole said with a smirk on his face.

"Have you been drinking?" Lena asked?

"No, dis a good riddle." Ole answered. "Listen, how far to da middle of a lake?"

"Vut lake? Are you sure you not been drinking?" Lena asked?

"Answer good for any lake, and I not been drinking?" Ole responded.

"I don't know, vut da answer?" Asked Lena.

"It tvice da distance to middle of Sven's forest?" Ole proudly answered.

"You dumkoff, dat don't make any sense," Lena shouted. "I know you been drinking. You get in da house."

As he went into the house, Ole was shaking his head, saying: "I don't understand, it make sense ven Sven say da riddle."

THE PRETTY GIRL

Sven and Ole one day took a walk
And along the way they did talk;
They stopped for a while,
As they both gave a smile
Toward a pretty girl to whom they did gawk!

As the girl was passing them by,
It was red-faced Ole who said, "Hi."
Sven gave a big wink
And his heart it did sink,
When he saw Helga, his wife, standing by.

She took Sven by the ear and yelled, "Look!
It's your goose I gonna cook!
You vink de eye
At da girl passing by,
So to me you yust be a snook!"

"But Helga," Sven said so sincere,
"Please let go of my ear,
It's not vat you tink
My eye it no vink,
Something in my eye brought a tear."

Ole, was taking this in,
To Sven he had a big grin
To Ole Helga said,
"You vish you ver dead
Ven I tell Lena your big sin!"

Now when Sven and Ole walk
They just continue to talk,
When a pretty girl comes by
Neither one gives the eye
And they never ever gawk!

HUNTING

Sven and Ole go hunting one day
Dressed up in their new hunting array
Thru the woods they did roam,
Forgetting rifles that were at home;
But their jackets were seen miles away.

BUY LOGS

Sven and Ole had decided to order a 10-cord truckload of logs for cutting. They had always ordered split wood before, so this was a new experience. Ole was on the phone with a logger.

"Yes, Mr. Logger, my neighbor Sven and me vant order some of dem logs. Now do ve pay extra to have de roots cut off? No? Dat's good."

"Vat about limbs?" Dey are cut off, too. Can ve save money if you deliver vid de limbs still on?"

"Sven, he says they don't deliver vid the limbs on. He's vondering if ve are pulling his legs."

Sven says, "Tell him ve only pull tabs, not legs."

Ole continued: "You deliver 10-cord at a time? How big of a cord do you use?"

"Sven, he say his cord is standard 128 cubic feet."

Sven grabs the phone, "Let me talk to dis guy."

"Say, Mr. Logger, ve don't know from cubic feet. Ve vant to know how big your rope is dat hold your logs togedder." Sven to Ole, "Now I know he not truthful. He say he don't use any ropes."

Ole to Sven, "Ask him vat kind of vood he has."

Sven on the phone, "Vat kind of vood do you have?" To Ole, "He say Oak, Maple, Birch, Poplar and a little Spruce. He say he can deliver a mix"

Sven on the phone, "Ve don't vant no mix. Ve vant half Oak, half Maple and de rest Poplar."

Sven to Ole, "He says ve are still pulling his leg and hung up."

"It's a good ting," says Ole, "Ve might have gotten a load vid no cord and some mix in dere."

A LIGHT YEAR

"Sven, how dey measure da distance in space?" Ole asked.

"Oh dey use a light year. Dat how far light go in von year," Sven answered.

"Uff da," Ole exclaimed, "dey able to measure speed of light?"

"Ya, dey know it go about 186 tousand mile per second," Sven answered.

"Dat fast, but I betcha speed of dark faster," Ole said.

"Vut you mean, speed of dark?" Sven asked, "Dere ain't no such ting."

"Dat cuz it so fast dey can't measure it," Ole proudly answered.

A TSUNAMI

"I see on TV dat dere vas an island dat vas hit by tsunami," Ole mentioned to Sven. "Vat dat tsunami anyvey?" Ole asked.

"Vell a tsunami is big, big vave dat happen ven big bunch of land fall into vater," Sven answered.

"Uff da," I see da tsunami and not even know it!" Ole exclaimed.

"Vere you ever see a tsunami?" Sven asked.

"Dat summer ven uncle Lars vas visiting and ve vent to da public swim pool to cool down," Ole answered. "Ven big Lars yump in pool, dere vas a big, big vave dat nearly emptied da pool!"

"I vouldn't call it a tsunami," Sven disagreed. "I'd call dat a Larsami."

"You betcha," Ole agreed, "a Larsami is da tsunami up close and personal!" They both laughed thinking about it.

ARK OF THE COVENANT

"You know, Ole, dat ark of da covenant vas quite a ting," Sven commented.

"Ya, it protected Israel sometime." Ole added.

"But only ven Israel vas obeying God," Sven commented. "Dere vas a time dat da ark vas taken by da Philistines."

"How dat possible?" Ole asked.

"Da sons of Eli, da high priest, ver bad and Eli didn't do anyting about it," said Sven. "So it say in 1 Samuel 4:11, God kill Eli two sons and let da Philistines take da ark."

"Uff da, dat mean da Philistines could use da ark against Israel!" Ole exclaimed.

"No. God didn't vant da Philistines to keep da ark so dey all got hemorrhoids," Sven said laughing.

"You mean it hurt ven dey sat down?" Ole laughed

"It hurt ven dey valk, too!" Sven roared. "Dey soon got God's message and gave back da ark."

"And dey limped all da vey back to dere village", Ole yelled, slapping Sven on the back, both laughing heartily at the thought.

AT THE BAR

Sven and Ole walk into a bar. Sven had been here before and explained that everyone orders a drink with an abbreviated code word. As they walked up to the bar, a patron ahead says, "Hey, give me an ML." The bartender nods his head and hands her a Miller Lite.

Sven walks up to the bartender and says, "I'd like a BL." Giving him a nod, the bartender pulls up a Bud Lite.

Finally Ole walks up to the bartender and says, "Give me a Fifteen."

"A Fifteen?" the bartender replies, "What in the world is that?"

"Oh, you know," Ole says, "A Seven and Seven."

DAYLIGHT SAVINGS TIME

Sven and Ole were talking about having to move their clocks ahead in the Spring.

"Vy ve need to change clocks anyvay?" Ole asked.

"Vell in Springtime, ven days get longer, by moving clocks ahead von hour, it mean most people up ven sun is up, saving electricity for lights. In evening, sunlight vun hour longer, saving electricity again," Sven explained.

"But day is still same length, right?" Ole asked.

"Yes, days are still 24 hours long," Sven replied.

Ole said, "It like cutting bottom off blanket and sewing to da top."

ATHLETE'S FEET

Ole just got back from his doctor and found he had athlete's foot. "I don't understand how I have da athlete's feet ven I don't even valk very much," Ole was telling Sven.

"It caused by a fungus," Sven commented. "You no need to be an athlete."

"Vell dat good," Ole said

"Vy dat good?" Sven asked.

"I don't need to start exercising to become an athlete." Ole said, quite relieved.

"It vouldn't hurt you to exercise and to put on some veight," Sven said.

"You tink I'm too skinny?" Ole asked.

"You so skinny. Ole, dat you need to stand in same place twice to make da shadow!" Sven roared.

BUCKING LOGS

Sven and Ole were having wood logs delivered so they could cut them up for firewood and save money instead of having split wood delivered. Their neighbor, Lars, told them they needed a chainsaw to buck the logs. With chainsaw in hand, they approached the pile of logs.

"You know, Sven," said Ole, "I know ve need to cut da logs into pieces for splitting, but vat is dis bucking stuff?"

"Oh, dat's nuttin', said Sven. "You seen da big buck deer how dey yump over tings."

"Yes," said Ole.

"Vell," continued Sven, "It's yust a vay of saying you need to toss dose pieces high ven somethin' is in da vay."

"You know, Sven, you pretty smart guy," said Ole.

"You betcha," said Sven. "My dad he said dat I had more brains in my little finger den in my whole head!"

"Your Dad vas right about dat, by golly," Ole added.

BUILDING A WOODSHED

Sven and Ole decide to build a woodshed. They ordered plans off the Internet and gathered all the material and tools they needed. The plans include blueprint and detailed instructions.

"Now dat ve have de foundation in, ve can start putting up da valls," says Ole.

"You betcha," says Sven. "And once da valls are up, we can put on da roof."

"You know, Sven," says Ole, "I'm glad ve decided to build dis ourselves."

"You betcha," says Sven. "Dis hole shed only cost us 700 bucks and two veeks to build."

"Yuh," says Ole, "Da guy down the road build sheds and he vas villing to build von for total cost of 700 bucks."

"It's a good thing ve didn't do it," says Sven, "Ve vould have missed out on all dis experience."

"By the vay, Sven," says Ole, "Vhat does it mean by Building Permit Required?"

CATCH A SKUNK

Sven calls up Ole and asks him to come over, he needs Ole's help.

"Vut you need my help vid," Ole asked when he saw Sven.

"I tell you bout da skunk dat been in my garden. Vell I set da trap and caught him last night," Sven told Ole.

"You mean you have da skunk out back by your garden?" Ole asked.

"Ya, an I need your help," Sven answered.

When Ole saw the skunk he said, "Dat da biggest skunk I ever seen!"

"Ya, an he pretty mad vid leg caught in trap," Sven remarked. "I heard dat if you lift up da hind legs, da skunk no can spray his stink."

"So vut your plan?" Ole asked.

"I vant you to stay in front of skunk and keep his attention vile I sneak up and lift him by da tail. Dat vay he not able to spray," Sven told Ole.

They both get into position and Sven begins to sneak up on the skunk. All at once, the skunk starts spraying Sven. Ole starts to laugh and he gets sprayed. As they walk to the barn to clean up Sven says, "I don't unnerstand how he know I behind him. I no make da noise."

"Maybe he have a Sven alarm," Ole said.

"Vutever he have, it sure vorks good," Sven said as they both started laughing.

CHANGEOUT PROGRAM

Sven and Ole heard about a program that provided incentives for people to get new more-efficient wood stoves or fireplace inserts by trading in their old ones. There wasn't any such program where they lived so they decided to start their own.

"You know, Sven," Ole was saying. "Ve need to come up vid someting so people vill trade dere ol stoves."

"Das da problem, Ole," Sven replied. "Ve don have nobody dat give money for ol stoves."

"Vell maybe ve hold da raffle for new stove and put money in bank, den we split money vid people in program," said Ole.

"Dat too much trouble," Sven remarked. "We yust tell people ve have von-year program but no money so dey have to changeout on dere own."

"Vat happens after von year is up?" asked Ole.

"After von year da program ends and ve can't help dem anymore." Said Sven.

CHIMNEY SWEEP

Ole was over visiting Sven one day and asked Sven, "You know Sven, I vas read da paper and I see dis ad for a chimney sveep; vy vood anyvon vant to have dere chimney svept?"

"Ole, da chimney sveep guy he have da special training and equipment to clean da chimney," said Sven.

Ole laughed, "Dat sound pretty funny, somevon up dere on da roof cleaning outside da chimney vid soap and vater."

"No, Ole, dey clean da inside. Dey get rid of da soot and creosote dat build up in dere," said Sven

"Uff da! Ver dat creosote come from?" asked Ole.

"Dat come from da vood dat burn too slow," said Sven. "Ven da vood green or dere not air to keep fire hot, den creosote show up. Da chimney sveep guy have da brush to clean inside da chimney."

"Okie dokie, smart guy, den vy dey called chimney sveep instead of chimney brush?" asked Ole.

"Tink about it, Ole," replied Sven. "Ven dey verk round chimney, it get dirty on roof, so dey sveep up before dey are done."

"Dat make good sense, by golly" replied Ole. "How come you so smart?"

"I alvays ben smart," Sven replied. "Ven I took da test in school I vas so smart all da other kids had to be twice as smart on da test yust to keep up!"

EXODUS

"You know, Ole, ven God did all dem miracles and brought da people of Israel out of Egypt," Sven was saying, "dat must have been someting to see!"

"Ya," Ole agreed. "Da pillar of fire musta been awesome."

"How about da vind dat separated da vater, dat hard to believe," Sven added.

"I don't know," Ole disagreed, "I seen da vind do some terrible ting."

"Vat da verst ting you see da vind do?" asked Sven.

"Vell, I remember ven Lena vas in da outhouse and da vind blew hard, it pushed dat outhouse vay out in da middle of da field," Ole remarked.

"Vat happen to Lena?" Sven asked. "Did she get hurt?"

"Nuttin happen. She vas busy reading da Sears catalog and didn't even know da outhouse moved!" Ole laughed.

"She took da trip vidout da car!" Sven roared.

FISHING BOAT

Sven and Ole rented a fishing boat and began fishing on a new lake for them. They tried several spots on the lake with no luck. Finally, they found a spot where they caught a lot of fish.

"Dis da best fishing ve ever have, Ole, it must be da rented boat," Sven said.

"Ya, ve never have luck like dis before," Ole agreed. "I mark da back of da boat vid chalk for next time.'

"Dat good, Ole, but da boat might be out next time and ve haf to rent other boat," Sven commented.

"I tought of dat, too," said Ole. "I mark da fishing spot vid some red string I lay on da vater."

FISHING IN CANADA

Sven and Ole had gone to Canada for a week to fish and ended up catching only one medium rainbow trout. On their way back to Minnesota, Sven said, “You know, Ole, dat von fish cost us $640.”

$640 for dat von little fish?” Ole asked.

“Ya, dat vut it cost for dis whole trip,” Sven remarked.

“Uff da, it good ting ve only caught von fish!” Ole commented.

“Ya, ve barely can afford dis one,” Sven agreed.

FITNESS CLUB

Sven and Ole join a fitness club and they arrive on their first day, ready to go.

“You know, Sven, dis club give each member a personal trainer,” Ole said as they entered the building.

“Dat silly, Ole, I not here to learn someting, I here to get da muscle,” Sven remarked.

A trainer greeted them at the door and took them to the beginner’s weight lifting area. “You boys are new here so we need to start you off slow and easy,” said the trainer.

Sven piped up, “Dat may be okay for Ole, here, but I don need no baby sitter for dese exercise. I verked vid da veights before.”

“That’s good,” replied the trainer. “How long did you work out and how big were the weights you were using?

“I use stuff round da farm dere. I vork out for two veeks den I qvit”, said Sven.

"What were you lifting?" asked the trainer.

"Oh I lift flakes of hay for horses and milk pail from da cow," said Sven.

"You mean bales of hay for the horses, don't you?" asked the trainer.

"Oh no, I break bale into flakes," said Sven.

"That's not much weight, said the trainer. "Let's see, a pail full of milk must weigh 15 or 20 pounds," said the trainer. "That's a pretty good weight to begin with."

"Oh, no," Sven corrected, "I don lift full pail, only about qvarter full!"

"I'm surprised you only got a quarter of a pail of milk from your cow," said the trainer.

"Oh, da cow, she give lots more milk dan dat, but full pail too heavy so I make lotsa trips," said Sven.

"That sounds very inefficient," said the trainer.

Ole piped in, "Dat ven his vife Olga found out and told him to lift whole bale of hay and fill up da pail all da vay."

Sven blurted, "Ven I found I had to do all dat verk, I qvit da job."

FOOL'S GOLD

Sven and Ole were very excited while visiting Alaska. They had just bought what they thought was gold at half price. They were at the Assayer's Office getting their so-called gold weighed. As soon as the Assayer saw their ore he said, "I hate to tell you guys this, but someone sold you 10 ounces of Fool's Gold. If this was real gold, at the going rate, it would be worth $1600."

"See Sven," Ole said, "Ve make da big profit. It only cost us $800 for dis stuff."

"But dis is Fool's Gold," Sven told Ole.

"It not a problem, Sven, ve go back and buy 10 more ounces to break even," Ole said.

"Ole you not very smart, if ve vant to make big profit ve need to buy 20 ounces or more," Sven commented.

GASIFICATION

Sven and Ole heard that their neighbor, Lars, just got a new outside wood furnace so they wandered over to see it. Lars came out and walked them to the back yard.

As they approached the back yard, Sven saw a small metal building and said, "Say, Lars, how come you got da fancy outhouse dere?"

Laughing, Lars, said, "No Sven, that's my new wood-burning furnace."

"Uff da," said Sven. "You be kiddin' us?" he asked.

"No," said Lars. This is one of the latest wood furnaces. It converts wood to gas and burns the gas at 2000 degrees. That, in turn, heats water that I use to heat my house, it gives me hot water for the kitchen and bathrooms, and it heats my barn."

"Uff da," said Ole. "You heat all dat from da vood?" he asked.

"Yes," Lars said. "It's a gasification furnace, it gives off very little smoke and I am using about 30% less wood."

"I know about dat gas stuff. It burn real good," said Ole.

"Hold on dere, Ole, How you know about gas burning?" asked Sven.

"Don't you remember at Aunt Olga's party last year ven Uncle Olaf ate too much of dat bean soup?" asked Ole. "Vell, he vas having da gas all over da place and got too close to da candles and burned a hole in his pants."

"Oh, yuh, I remember," said Sven. "You are right, dat gas stuff burn pretty good, by golly"

GIVING THE BRIDE AWAY

Ole's oldest daughter was getting married and Ole was putting on his new suit while Sven was helping him. "Dis is very special day for you, Ole" Sven said.

"You betcha," Ole responded. "But I no like to vare da monkey suit."

"You look good in da monkey suit," Sven commented. "Besides, not every day you give avay da bride."

"Oh, no, Sven, I no give avay da bride," Ole insisted, "Her fiancé, he have good dowry."

GOLIATH

"You know, Ole, dat Goliath vas von big guy," Sven remarked.

"You betcha, Sven," Ole answered, "He vas about 10 feet tall!"

"Dat some big pair of britches," Sven said as he gestured with his arms. "He challenged da Israelite army for somevon to fight him. Everyvon in Israeli army scared to fight until David come by."

"Ya and David vas but a teenage boy," Ole added.

"But David not afraid because he believe God vould help him," Sven said, "and He did. Ven David use da sling, da rock hit Goliath on da forehead and knocked him down."

"Dat big giant vent down to da ground like da big tree," Ole said

"Den David ran to da giant, took da giant's sword and cut off his head," Sven remarked.

"Dat pretty smart of David, vid giant's head cut off giant couldn't fight any more," Ole remarked.

"Ya, because da giant dead," Sven added.

"No," Sven, "because giant can't see vere David is vid head cut off:" Ole pointed out.

GONE SKIING

Sven, Helga, Ole and Lena are on vacation at a ski resort when Lena complained to her Ole that she needed to go to the restroom. He told her not to worry, that he was sure there was an outhouse at the top. He was wrong, of course, and the pain did not go away.

Ole, realizing she was in pain, said, "You go behind da trees and vid your vite outfit and da snow you not be seen."

So Lena went beyond the tree line, lowering her ski pants and proceeded to do her thing.

Without warning, Lena found herself skiing backward, out-of-control, racing through the trees. Her bottom was still bare, and she was picking up speed.

She continued back under the lift, and finally collided with a small tree. The bad news was that she broke her arm and was unable to pull up her ski pants. Ole arrived, put an end to her nudie show, then summoned the ski patrol.

While Lena was in the emergency room, a man with an obviously broken leg was put in the bed next to hers.

"So, how'd you break your leg?" Lena asked.

"It was the darndest thing you ever saw", he said. "I was riding up this ski lift and suddenly I couldn't believe my eyes. There was this crazy woman skiing backward out-of-control, down the mountain, with her bare bottom hanging out of her clothes and her pants down around her knees. I leaned over to get a better look and fell out of the lift."

GRAVEN IMAGE

"I didn't know, ve not supposed to draw image of a tombstone," Ole was telling Sven.

"Vut you mean?" asked Sven

"In Exodus 20:4 it say thou shalt not make any graven image," Ole replied.

"No, Ole, dat not vut it mean," Sven responded. "It mean ve not make any image of an idol to vership. Ve are only to vership God."

"Den vut dat have to do vid da grave?" Ole asked.

"No," Ole, "not grave, it say graven. Dat like an engraving," Sven said.

"Now dat make sense," Ole replied. "How come you so smart, Sven?"

"It because I have so much brain I haven't used yet," Sven answered. My teacher used to tell me I not use much of my brain," Sven agreed.

GREEN WOOD

Sven and Ole set up the foundations for their windrows and began stacking their split pieces of wood.

"You know, Sven," said Ole. If ve hadn't read da vood book, ve vould be stacking dis vood against da barn or someting."

"You betcha," said Sven. "Maybe even against da house."

"Dose vindrows dey make sense," said Ole. "Ve stack vere da wind she blow."

"You betcha, and vere da sun she shine," said Sven.

"Vun ting I don't understand," said Ole. "It's da green vood. Ve ben cuttin' all summer and I don't see no green vood."

"Oh," said Sven, "Dats an insider vay of saying dat da vood is vet."

"Den vy don't dey say vet instead of green?" asked Ole.

"It like da code ting," answered Sven. "Remember in school ven you vanted to go to the bathroom, you used a code like number 1 or number 2. Dis is like dat."

"So da vood go to bathroom?" Ole asked.

"No," Sven laughed, "It yust ven da tree be cut down, da vood is vet from da sap."

"Dat must be da same sap dat cause da trouble in school," said Ole.

"Never mind," Sven says as he walks away in frustration.

HELPING A TOURIST

Sven and Ole were out walking one day when a big car drives by their gravel road. The car stops and the man inside lowers his window and yells to the two of them, "Say, I'm kinda lost and was wondering how I get to Hinkley. I am meeting my family there at the casino."

Sven and Ole looked at each other, rubbed their chins and thought a while. Finally, Sven yells to the stranger, "You pretty lost alright. You no can get to casino from here. You need to go back down da road dere an get to corner vere Lars Larsen use to live. Take da right turn an go to Mora. Vhen you get to Mora, den you follow sign to Hinkley."

"That seems a roundabout way of getting there. Why can't I go directly from here?" asked the stranger.

Sven and Ole laughed hard. When they caught their breath, Ole yelled: "Cause dere a sign to Hinkley in Mora. Dere ain't no sign here."

HOW MANY DEAD

Sven and Ole were driving to town when they started passing a cemetery. Sven pointed at the cemetery and asked, "How many people dead in dat cemetery, Ole?"

"Dat pretty big cemetery," Ole responded, dere may be a hundred or more. I don't know, you know, Sven?"

"Ya, I know…dey all dead," Sven laughed.

"You got me on dat one, Sven," Ole laughed.

About a week later they were travelling a different road when Ole saw a cemetery up ahead. Eager to get back at Sven, Ole blurted out: "I know how many dead in dat cemetery coming up"

"How many?" Sven asked.

"All of dem," shouted Ole, feeling proud of himself.

As they drove by the cemetery, Sven said, "I don't tink so."

Ole looks where Sven is pointing and sees two men with shovels digging a grave.

HOW TO CATCH A RABBIT

"Sven, I have foolproof vay to catch da rabbit," Ole remarked.

"Oh? Vut you foolproof vay?" Sven asked.

"It easy, ven you see rabbit yust make sound like da carrot." Ole responded proudly.

"Dat funny, Ole," Sven said. "Now I ask you, vut easy vay to catch da polar bear?"

"I don't tink dere easy vay," Ole replied, "But I ask anyvay."

"Vell," Sven said smiling, "you cut a big hole in da ice and sprinkle can of peas all round da hole. Ven da bear come to take a pea, you hit him in da ice-hole."

HOW TO LAND ON THE SUN

Sven and Ole were talking about all the discoveries made in outer space lately.

"You know, Ole, you tink dey vould figure out how to land on da sun," Sven said.

"Oh, I gut dat all figured out," Ole replied.

"Vut, you know how to land on da sun?" Sven asked.

"You betcha," Ole answered. "It be simple," Ole answered, "Dey land at night."

"Dat vont verk," Ole. "It be too dark to see," Sven reasoned.

"I have dat figured out too, Sven, dey bring some big flashlights," Ole answered.

"Uff da, an lotsa batteries," Sven added.

HUNTING

One day, Lars, Sven and Ole go hunting. Lars is a very good hunter, so Sven and Ole plan to watch him. They arrive at the hunting cabin, and get all set up. The next day, Lars goes out. He returns with a big deer. Sven and Ole ask him how he did that. They can't believe how big the deer is.

"It vas easy," Lars explained. "I found da tracks, followed da tracks, and BAM shot the deer."

The next day, Sven goes out, and comes back with an even bigger deer. Ole's eyes bug out when he sees it, and he asks Sven how he did it.

"Same ting as Lars. I find da tracks, followed da tracks, and BAM shot the deer."

On the third day, Ole goes hunting. He doesn't come back for a very long time. When he staggers into the cabin, rifle gone, all beat up and bruised, with only one boot, Lars and Sven ask Ole what happened.

"Vell…I find da tracks, and follow da tracks, Ole said. "BAM got run over by da train."

LOG SPLITTERS

Ole was trying to get Sven to share the cost of a log splitter but Sven didn't want to do it.

"Come on Sven, ve can save de time vid de log splitter," Ole was saying.

"How dat save time?" Sven asked. "Our logs dey be 8 feet long. If ve split dem, dey still 8 feet long."

"No, Sven," Ole replied. "De log splitter is to split dose pieces ve cut from dose logs. Dose pieces dey also called logs"

"Dat don't make no sense at all. Dey should call dem piece splitters," said Sven in disgust.

"You right, Sven," replied Ole, "But dey probly vouldn't sell too many vid a name like dat."

MAKING A LEVERAGE POLE

"You know, Sven, ve need to make da leverage pole," Ole exclaims. "Ve got a load of dem logs comin' and ve need da pole."

"You betcha, Ole," "dem pole dey come handy ven ve need to roll da log down da pile," says Sven. "Ve have da small fence post, maybe dat verk for us."

"You go find da pole and I find da pole," says Ole, "Den ve make two dem poles."

When Sven shows up, Ole had already found a pole and cut a wedge-shaped end. He looks at Sven and sees him carrying a small pole and a big pole.

"Vy you have da two poles dere, Sven?" Ole asks, "You only need von pole, not two."

"Vel," says Sven, "I tot about dat and know ve need two poles, von for da little log and von for da big log."

"Vy do you have da vedge cut on both end of da poles?" asked Ole, "Don you need only von vedge?"

"You see, Ole, dat vere I be smart," Sven remarks proudly. "Vid your pole if you pick up by end vid vedge, you no can use. Vid my pole I can use no matter vut end I pick up."

MAN CAVE

"Say, Sven, I tinking of making a place to vatch sports," Ole said.

"You don't have room, ver you do dis?" Sven asked.

"Vell, I hear dat some guys dey make place in da garage," Ole replied.

"Oh, ya, dey make da man cave," Sven commented.

"No vay! I no make da cave," Ole responded.

"Vy you no make da cave?" Sven asked.

"Ve live in Minnesota. I no vant bear to come in my cave!" Ole exclaimed.

MANNEQUINS

"I see dem changing da clothes on da store dummies down town," Ole was telling Sven.

"Ya, dey call manekins," Sven replied.

"I don't see no manekins," Ole replied emphatically.

Sven laughed, "Doze dummies in da store, vut vould you call dem?"

"Dey not manekins for sure," Ole said, "dey had da long hair and breast; dat no manekin! I vould call dem vomenekins."

MENTAL HYGIENE

"You know, Sven, I read dat doing puzzles is good mental hygiene. Vat dat mean?" Ole asked.

"Dat like exercise for da brain," Sven answered. "It make da brain verk better."

"You so smart, Sven, you must do lot of mental hygiene," Ole commented.

"No, I ben smart all my life," Sven said. "Ven I vas in grade school I vas so smart teacher sent me back von grade to help other kids."

"Dat really someting," Ole remarked.

"You betcha," Sven added, "da teacher say vid me around, kids need all da help dey can get!"

MT. RUSHMORE

"You know, Sven," said Ole as he, Sven and their wives were looking at the presidential carvings on Mt. Rushmore, "Da view here of da presidents is someting, by golly."

"You betcha," replied Sven, "an it real lucky dat dis place happen to be here, you know."

"Ya," said Ole, "before da president carving, dis place don have much business."

Ole's wife Lena pipes up, "Uff da, you guys, dis place vas built after da carvings."

"How you know dat, smarty pants," Ole said, teasingly.

"Oh, it vas hard to guess, since da plaque says da whole history," Lena answered.

As they left, Sven was driving and missed the turn back on the main highway.

His wife, Olga, shouted, "You yust missed da main highvay."

"No," said Sven, "I take da road to back side of Mt. Rushmore."

Everyone shouted in unison, "Vy you vant go backside of da mountain?"

Sven says, "Ve see how dey did good job on president faces, I vanna see how good back of da heads look."

OLDEST MAN IN THE WORLD

"Say, Sven, I didn't know anyvon could live for 50 tousand years?" Ole asked.

"No, Ole, da oldest man dat ever live vas Metuselah. He live for 969 years. Vere you get dis 50 tousand year ting?" Sven asked.

"I read in da paper, dey dug up bone of man dat vas 50 tousand years old," Ole replied.

Sven laughed, "dat mean he live 50 tousand year ago."

"How dey know it vas 50 tousand year ago?" Ole asked.

"Dat call carbon dating and measure long times," Sven answered.

"Ya, I remember ven I date girl in high school. She vas a terrible date and it seem to last a long, long time," Ole laughed.

MUSHROOM MANAGEMENT

"I read da article dat a lot of companies having employee problems," Ole told Sven.

"Ya, Ole. Lots of companies practice mushroom management," Sven replied.

"Vut dat mushroom management?" Ole asked.

"Dat vare management keep da employees in da dark, cover dem vid manure, and ven dey start to grow, dey can dem," Sven answered.

NOAH'S FLOOD

"You know, Ole, I vas reading in da Bible about Noah's flood," Sven said.

"Ya, dat vas some rain storm!" Ole agreed. "Can you imagine two of every animal on da ark? Dey must have had good air conditioning."

"Vat you mean, good air conditioning?" asked Sven.

"Vell, dere must have been good air conditioning, dere vas two skunks on board." Ole commented.

"Uff da, you so right, Ole," Sven said with surprise. "Maybe dey have two skunks vid no stink."

"Or Noah and his family have colds and can't smell," Ole said, laughingly.

OLE TAKES A SWIM

The weather was very hot and Ole wanted desperately to take a dive in a nearby lake. He didn't bring his swimsuit, but he was all alone, so he undressed and got into the water.

After a while, a pair of old ladies walked onto the shore in his direction. He panicked, got out of the water and grabbed a bucket lying in the sand nearby. He strategically positioned the bucket and sighed with relief.

The ladies got nearby and looked at him. He felt awkward and wanted to move. Then one of the ladies said: "You know, I have a special gift, I can read minds…"

"Impossible", said Ole, "You really know vat I tink?"

"Yes", the lady said with a grin, "In fact, right now, I bet you think that the bucket you're holding has a bottom."

OLE TAKES PIANO LESSONS

Sven continued to play the piano from his childhood and became good at it. One day Ole came over to visit Sven while Sven was playing the piano.

When Sven was done playing, Ole said, "You play good, Sven. I vish I could play like dat."

Sven looked at Ole and said, "you can learn to play, Ole, and you don't need to buy expensive piano."

"Vat I play on if not da piano?" Ole asked.

"Oh, dey have da keyboards dat only cost a few hundred dollars. You could learn to play on von of dem, "Sven replied."

Ole thought about it and asked if Sven would come with him to pick out a keyboard, to which Sven agreed.

After playing a few different keyboards, Sven recommended a particular one which was on sale and had six free lessons during the trial period. If Ole didn't like the keyboard for any reason during the 30-day trial period, he could return it and get all of his money back.

Sven helped Ole set up his keyboard at home and played a couple of tunes on it to check it out.

"You have two free lessons a veek so you should be doing pretty good by da end of da 30 days trial," Sven commented.

"Ya, an soon I be playing da music," Ole said with delight.

About three weeks later Sven happened to see Ole in town and asked how the music lessons were going.

"Oh, I returned da keyboard after tree lessons," Ole remarked.

"But dat vas such a nice keyboard," Sven said.

"Oh, da keyboard vas fine, but after tree lessons, da teacher gave up." Ole announced.

"Vy da teacher give up?" Sven asked.

"She say I no play on da keys, I play in da cracks!" Ole said.

OLE'S EYE PROBLEM

Sven saw Ole in a down mood. "Vat wrong vid you, Ole, you sorta draggin your feet today?" Sven asked.

"Oh, I vent to da eye doctor and he gave me some bad news," Ole replied.

"Vut bad news is dat?" Sven asked.

"Da doctor say I have ocular degeneration," Ole responded.

"Dat sound bad, all right," Sven agreed. "Did he say how long you have to live?" Sven asked.

"Dat da problem, Sven, I could go blind and not see da end coming," Ole answered.

"Dat bad, all right, you be dead and not even know it!" Sven commented.

OLE'S FAVORITE COLOR

Sven wanted to get Ole a present for his birthday and wanted to wrap it in paper of Ole's favorite color.

"Vut your favorite color?" Sven asked Ole.

"Vy you vant to know?" Ole asked in return.

"I vant to wrap your present vid paper dat your favorite color," Sven replied.

"Vell, you vill have to guess." Ole said with a smile.

"Okay, is it blue, red or green?" Sven asked?

"No," Ole answered, getting a kick out of the proceeding.

Sven continues rattling off colors with Ole saying no to each one.

"Look, Ole, I say all da colors of da rainbow and still you say no, so I give up," Sven stated.

"In a cheerful voice, Ole said, "I knew you vouldn't guess it. My favorite color is plaid."

OLE'S MEMORY PROBLEM

Ole had been having trouble remembering things. He heard about a one-week-long memory improvement seminar conducted by a world-famous psychiatrist. He had just got back from the seminar and Sven was eager to talk to him about it. They were walking together and their wives were walking ahead when Sven asked, "How did da memory seminar go, Ole?"

"Sven, it vas da best ting I ever did," Ole replied. "Ve do all kinds of exercise to improve memory. It vas fun and also very good seminar."

"So you say dat your memory better?" Sven asked.

"You betcha," answered Ole, with conviction.

"Da teacher of seminar a very famous psychiatrist?" Sven asked.

"Oh he verld famous," Ole replied. "He go all over da verld teaching"

"Vut da teacher name? I may vant to go to seminar," Sven commented.

"Vy he doctor...doctor," Ole pauses, then yells to Lena. "Say, Lena, vut da name of dat doctor dat teach da memory seminar?"

OLE'S OUTHOUSE

Ole's cabin had an outhouse that needed replacing. He wanted the new one to be a two-seater but there wasn't the room to expand out without knocking down some nice trees. He mentioned his problem to Sven for his ideas.

Sven said, "You have nice trees dere. I don't see any vay you make two-seater vidout cutting down trees."

Ole thanked him for his input and went back to his cabin to think about it.

A couple of weeks later, Sven saw Ole and asked if he completed the outhouse.

"You betcha," Ole replied, "and it a two seater, too."

Sven asked, "How many trees did you have to cut down?"

"Oh, dat the good part, I no cut any trees," Ole replied.

"How you make two-seater vidout cutting trees?" Sven asked.

"It vas simple. I make da outhouse two story!" Ole exclaimed, with pride.

OLE'S WRESTLING MATCH

When Sven and Ole were in their teens, Ole joined the high school wrestling team. He had been working out for months and was very strong. His first match was a practice against a foreign team. The coach wanted to simplify things so he told the competitors that if either wanted to end the match, all they had to do was yell the word sufficient.

Sven was on the sidelines yelling support to Ole as the match progressed. Right off, Ole's opponent gets him in a headlock. Ole's face turns red but he wriggles out of the hold. A minute later the opponent has Ole in a painful back bend. Ole's face turns red again, but still says nothing. Sven is getting concerned for his friend when Ole manages to get out of the hold and reverses it on his opponent. Immediately, the opponent cries out: "Sufficient."

Ole looks at the coach and exclaims: "Dat's da verd I been trying to tink of all dis time!"

ONION CONDITION

Ole was coming out of the doctor's office when Sven spotted him. Sven asked Ole what he found out from the doctor.

"Vell, I know vy my feet smell," Ole said.

"Dat good to know, now you can do something about it," Sven commented. "Vat da cause of da smell?

"Da doctor says I have an onion condition," Ole replied.

Laughing, Sven says, "You have an onion condition? Are you sure?"

"Dat vut I heard him say," Ole insisted.

"Let me see your papers from da doctor," Sven demanded. Looking through the papers, Sven starts laughing.

"Vut so funny dere Sven?" Ole asked

"You funny. Doctor no say you have onion, he say you have bunion!" Sven laughed even louder.

OSTRICH

Ole and Sven were talking one day and Ole said he read where ostriches put their heads in sand when they get scared.

Sven laughed, and said, "Dat old vives tale. Ostrich no put head in sand ven he afraid, dat silly."

"Vut ostrich do ven dey get scared, run to dere momma?" Ole asked laughingly.

"To make enemy disappear all dey need to do is close dere eyes," Sven proudly announced.

OVERHANG

Sven and Ole were arguing one day about splitting wood. Ole was explaining that a piece should not overhang the splitting block.

"Dat piece you have dere, Sven, is over de edge of de block," Ole warned. "Da vood book say not to split ven vood hang over de edge like dat."

"Oh, my gosh. Is dat vat da book say?" asked Sven.

"Yup, right dere in de chapter on safety vere he talk about da overhang," replied Ole.

Sven began laughing loudly and said, "You know, Ole, I tot he vas saying don't split vid a hangover!"

Both laughed and Ole added, "Dat probly good advice too!"

OXYMORON

"I read vere somevon said dat military intelligence vas an oxymoron," Ole was telling Sven. "Vat dat oxymoron mean?"

"Dat mean ven you use two vurds togeddere dat mean da opposite," answered Sven.

"So if I say handsome Sven, dat vould be oxymoron," Ole laughed.

"Ya, just like if I say smart Ole," Sven roared.

REROOFING

Sven and Ole got a job to reroof a neighbor's house. After tearing off the old roofing and placing an underlayment, they began nailing on shingles. Sven had placed a bundle of shingles near Ole for him to start while he brought up more bundles. Sven could hear the nails being pounded as he took another bundle from the ground and started up the ladder. As he slowly climbed, the nail pounding would stop for a while then begin again. When he reached the top of the ladder, he saw Ole pull out a nail from a box, look at it, throw it away, then pull out another nail, which he pounded into the shingle. Intrigued, Sven watched and again saw Ole throw away a couple of nails.

"Vy you trow avay nail from box?" Sven asked.

"Doze nails pointing wrong vay." Ole replied.

"Don't trow doze avay," Sven exclaimed. "Doze pointing wrong vay are for da udder side of roof."

PENTECOST

On their way out of church, Sven and Ole were talking about the day's sermon on the Pentecost.

"Dat must have been someting to see, Ole, all dem people togedder vating for da Holy Spirit," Sven commented.

"You betcha," Ole replied. "but I don't understand how dey got 120 people in von Honda!"

"Vut you mean, in von car? Dere vas nuting about a car." Sven said, shaking his head.

"Don't you remember, da minister read from Acts 2:1, dey ver all vid one accord in one place." Ole responded.

"Uff da, You right, Ole," Sven replied in disbelief. "Dat Honda Accord must have been a stretch limo!"

SEASONING WOOD

"You know, Sven, Da vood book ve bought talk about seasoning. You know vat dat mean?"

"You betcha," replied Sven. "Dat not same ting as Lena put in food. Dis a new kinda seasoning."

"So ven ve talk about food ben seasoned, dis not same ting?" asked Ole.

"You got dat right, by golly, Ole," replied Sven. "Ven dey say season for da vood, it come from two verds: da sea and da son."

"So season of da vood come from da verd sea and da verd son, dey put togedder?" asked Ole.

"You betcha," Sven replied. "Da sea part mean dat dere a wind like on da sea, and da son part dere dey mean sun like in sky. So togedder dey mean wood out vere vind blow and da sun shine."

"You pretty smart guy, Sven," says Ole.

"You betcha," said Sven. "Ven God gave out brain I told Him I vas already too smart so he give my brain to somebody else."

SELLING TOMATOES

Sven and Ole bought a pickup load of tomatoes from a local farmer for a dollar a pound. They set up a roadside stand and were selling them for seventy-five cents a pound. Lars, a neighbor of theirs came by and bought some tomatoes.

"Dees are good tomatoes," Lars commented. "Vere you get dem?"

Sven said, "Ve got dem from da farmer up da road. Ve pay a dollar a pound."

"If you sell dem for seventy-five cents, how you make any money?" Lars asked.

"Oh, ve make it up in volume," Sven answered. "Sales ben so good, Ole back at da farm buying more tomatoes."

SPLITTING WOOD

Sven and Ole had a lot of wood pieces cut from logs and were ready to start splitting.

"Say, Ole," Sven said, "Good ting ve read da vood book, ve have da place all set to split da vood."

"You know, Sven, it feel good to split da vood," said Ole.

"You betcha," said Sven. "Dat splitting make for da big muscles."

"You got dat right, by golly, Sven," said Ole, in agreement.

"Ven I start da splitting, I had hard time to hold up de axe," said Sven. "Now I can hold up two axes and sometimes even a maul!"

"Me too," said Ole. "And da vood pieces ve can lift are getting bigger, too."

"Yes, yust dis morning I pick up a six-incher all by myself," exclaimed Sven.

"I bet if ve keep dis up, by da end of da summer ve vill be able to tackle dose big twelve-inchers," said Ole, with excitement.

"Da real test, dough" said Sven, "is ven ve can use da maul to split da vood!"

ST. PETER

Sven was telling Ole that he had a dream the night before where he had died and was talking to St. Peter outside the Golden Gates of Heaven.

"You talk to St. Peter?" Ole asked.

"Ya he vouldn't let me in until I came back an make up to you for all da times I say you not smart," Sven replied.

"Dat sound very good," Ole said. "How you gonna make up to me?"

"Vell, I tought and tought about it and decided I have no more dream about St. Peter," Sven answered.

STACKING WOOD

Sven and Ole were nearly done with stacking their wood and were admiring their work.

"You know, Sven," said Ole, "Dis stacking is like da jigsaw puzzle."

"You betcha," said Sven. "You gotta find da right piece to keep da stack straight."

"I vonder if ve could invent some kinda machine dat vould straighten out de pieces," asked Ole

"You mean put in a crooked piece and out come a straight von?" Sven asked.

"Yup." Ole replied. "It vould make every piece straight so da stack she never lean and fall."

"Dat a good idea," said Sven. "De problem is it vould need a long, long extension cord."

"Yuh," agreed Ole. "Dat vould not be very smart. Maybe ve could invent vay to make paper from da vood."

"Dat crazy, Ole. Da vood vay too tick to do dat," Sven said, shaking his head.

THE BIG BANG

"You know, Ole, dem scientists say dat da whole universe, it started vid a big bang," Sven said.

"Vut you mean a big bang?" Asked Ole.

"Vell, dem scientist tink dat da universe vas a tiny, tiny ting, called a singularity, dat exploded," replied Sven.

"You mean ve have dis whole universe from a tiny singularity? Asked Ole.

"Dat's vut dey tink," answered Sven.

"Uff da," said Ole, shaking his head. "It's a good ting it vas only a singularity and not a doublearity! Who knows vat ve vould have!"

"You right, Ole, vid a doublearity dere might be two of everybody!" Sven said. "Dat vould be confusing!"

"You so right, Sven," Ole agreed. "If dere vas two Svens, I vouldn't know vich von vas you!"

STREAMING VIDEO

"Say, Sven, I hear dat Lars can vatch a movie on his IPad," Ole said.

"Ya, dat pretty nice. People can vatch movie from Internet on dere TV, IPad, Nook, and udder tings," Sven remarked. "It call streaming video. You should get dat."

"Streaming video?" Ole asked. "I couldn't vatch no streaming video," Ole said dejectedly.

"Vy not, Ole?" Sven asked.

"Because my vaderes have big hole in dem," Ole said, shaking his head.

SVEN GETS A NEW WOOD STOVE

Sven bought a new wood stove made of beautiful green soapstone. It had been delivered and installed. Ole, next door, watched as the installers drove away. He was eager to see the new stove so he walked over to Sven's house. He saw Sven through the door window searching around the door area. Sven saw Ole and beckoned him to come in.

"I come to see da new stove," Ole said.

"Ya, it a beauty, but dere a part missing and I need you to help me find it before Helga comes home," Sven replied. "I been looking all over and I cannot find da part.

"Vut part is missing?" Ole asked. "Vut does it look like?"

"Dat da trouble, Ole, I don't know vut it look like. But da salesman mention it two or tree times, so it must be important," Sven replied.

"Vell, vut dis part called?" Ole asked.

"Da salesman said dat dis stove had ambiance," Sven replied.

"Dat sound important to me," Ole remarked. "You better call da store and see if it still dere.

SVEN PIANO PLAYING

When Sven and Ole were in school, Sven was taking lessons to play piano. The room was very large with six pianos in it. The music teacher had six students and would have each student perform an exercise, one after another. It was nearing the end of their first year so the teacher wanted them all to compete by having them all play The Minute Waltz and see who came closest to performing the waltz in one minute.

Sven was the first to complete the waltz; he did it in 57 seconds. The other competitors required more than a minute; the longest was a minute and fifteen seconds. The teacher was amazed at Sven's speed.

Ole stopped by to listen and approached Sven and said, "Dat vos pretty fast playing dere Sven. How come you so fast?"

Sven looked at Ole and said, "I so fast dat everyvon else have to play twice as fast to keep up!"

SVEN RUNS FOR MAYOR

"You know, Ole," said Sven, "I tink I gonna run for da Mayor job."

"Vy not, Sven," said Ole, "you fit right in vid da other people."

"Dat vut I tot so too. I can mess tings up as good as dose people," Sven said laughing.

"Okey dokey, Sven, vat platform you run on?" Ole asked.

"Oh, I don need no platform," Sven answered. "I can stan on ground or on stage, it don matter to me."

"No, Sven, by platform dat mean vat you stan for? Vat you gonna do for da people?" Ole said.

"Oh, I gonna do lotsa tings, you betcha," Sven says. "I gonna fix all da street in town, I gonna get new school for da kids and I gonna take away all da taxes."

"Dat very good platform," Ole says. "You make lotsa promises but how you gonna pay for all dese tings?"

"Oh, I don pay dese tings, I yust make da promises," Sven answered.

"You know, Sven, you already sound like da politicians," Ole remarked.

THE BOOK OF JOB

"Vut you tink of dat guy, Job?" asked Sven.

"He vas some guy," Ole commented. "Even his friends blamed him."

"Ya, but vut most people don't know is von of his friends vas da shortest man in da verld," Sven replied.

"Vut friend you talking about?" asked Ole.

"It say in Job 2:11 dat von of his friends vos Bildad da Shuhite," Sven replied. "Now if dat not short I don't know vut is!"

"Uff da, only as high as a shoe?" Ole asked. "Dat really short. Ben better if he vos a Boot-height, don't you tink?" Ole asked.

"You betcha," Sven said as they both laughed about the thought.

VISIT QUEBEC

Sven and Ole were traveling with their wives in Canada. One of their stops was an overnight in Quebec. As they were continuing their travel the next day, they discussed the sights and foods of Quebec. Ole finally said, "You know vat impressed me da most?"

"You mean da food?" Lena asked.

"How about da friendly people, yust like Minnesota?" Helga asked.

"It musta ben da Old Quebec ve visited dis morning," Sven guessed.

"No, Ole responded, "it da people from Quebec; Dey must be da smartest people in da verld!"

"Vy you say dat?" Sven asked.

"Vell, I no can speak da French but I hear some two and tree year old kids speak da French!" Ole exclaimed.

THE GARDEN OF EDEN

"I vas tinking about da Garden of Eden," said Sven. "How nice it must have been."

"Ya," replied Ole, "da vedder vas nice all da time."

"And Adam named all dem animals," Sven added.

"Ya, and dey valked each day vid God," Ole said.

"Did you hear da joke about da snakes complaining to God?" Sven asked.

"You mean in da Garden of Eden?" asked Ole.

"Ya, a couple of snakes ver complaining to God," Sven continued. "God asked vhy dey ver complaining. Da snakes said to God dat you told us to multiply, but ve are only adders."

"Dat funny," Ole laughed. "Maybe dey get an adder machine to speed tings up."

THE GRAND TETONS

Sven and Ole were traveling with their wives in the western U.S. when they stopped to look at mountains in the distance.

"You know, Ole, dose mountains called da Grand Tetons," Sven said.

"Ya, I see da sign but vut dat mean?" Ole asked.

"Vell some French explorers ver here long time ago and ven dey saw da shape of da mountain it look like two big breasts," Sven answered.

"I no see big breasts," Ole responded.

"Vell, it take some imagination," Sven commented, "Remember da Frenchmen ver out here for months at a time. Dey probably tinking of da vomen dey missed."

"If it ver me," Ole said, "I vould be missing da soft bed."

"Ya, but vut kinda landmark vould Soft Bed be?" Sven laughed.

THE LONGEST WORD

"I know vut da longest verd in da dictionary," Ole said to Sven.

"How you know dat?" Sven asked.

"Somevon told me," Ole responded.

"Vell, den tell me…vut da longest verd?" Sven asked.

"It da verd smiles…dere's a mile betveen da esses," Ole proudly answered.

Lars was standing by and said, "Dat funny, Ole, but the longest verd in most large dictionaries is: pneumonoultramicroscopicsilicovolcanoconiosis, vich is a lung disease.